THE MAGIC OF LANGUAGE

Nouns

dog

eye

spot

nose

smile

mouth

paw

By Ann Heinrichs

THE CHILD'S WORLD®
CHANHASSEN, MINNESOTA

Published in the United States of America by The Child's World®
PO Box 326, Chanhassen, MN 55317-0326
800-599-READ
www.childsworld.com

Content Adviser:
Kathy Rzany, M.A.,
Adjunct Professor,
School of Education,
Dominican University,
River Forest, Illinois

Photo Credits: Cover photograph: Punchstock/Digital Vision Interior photographs:
Animals Animals/Earth Scene: 24 (Viola's Photo Visions, Inc.), 26 (Gerlach Nature
Photography); Corbis: 5 (Alan Schein Photography), 10, 11, 13 (Karl Ammann), 15
(Otto Rogge); Getty Images: 9 (PhotoDisc), 17 (National Geographic/Raymond K.
Gehman), 19 (The Image Bank/Ross Whitaker), 29 (Brand X Pictures); Getty
Images/Stone: 7 (Tim Davis), 8 (Peter Cade), 14 (James Cotier); Picture Finders
Ltd./eStock Photo/PictureQuest: 21.

The Child's World®: Mary Berendes, Publishing Director

Editorial Directions, Inc.: E. Russell Primm, Editorial Director; Pam Rosenberg,
Project Editor; Melissa McDaniel, Line Editor; Katie Marsico, Assistant Editor; Matt
Messbarger, Editorial Assistant; Susan Hindman, Copyeditor; Susan Ashley and Sarah E.
De Capua, Proofreaders; Chris Simms and Olivia Nellums, Fact Checkers; Timothy
Griffin/IndexServ, Indexer; Cian Loughlin O'Day and Dawn Friedman, Photo
Researchers; Linda S. Koutris, Photo Selector

The Design Lab: Kathleen Petelinsek, Design and Page Production;
Kari Thornborough, Page Production Assistant

Library of Congress Cataloging-in-Publication Data
Heinrichs, Ann.
  Nouns / by Ann Heinrichs.
      p. cm. — (The magic of language)
Includes index.
Contents: What is a noun?—Common and proper nouns—One or more than one?—
Watch out for Y!—Tricky plurals—More tricky plurals—Can you count them?—Where
is that gaggle?—When are two nouns better than one?—Get that energy off my foot!
  ISBN 1-59296-065-0 (library bound : alk. paper)
  1. English language—Noun—Juvenile literature. [1. English language—Noun.]
I. Title. II. Series: The Magic of Language.
  PE1201.H37 2004
  428.2—dc22   2003020035

Table of Contents

CHAPTER ONE

WHAT IS A NOUN?

DEFINITION

A **noun** is a naming word. It's the name of a person, place, or thing.

What is your name? What is your teacher's name? What is your best friend's name? All those names are nouns. They are names of people.

Jason, Clare, and **Mr. Primm** are all nouns. **Girl, grandma,** and **policeman** are nouns, too. They are also names for people.

Where do you live? Let's say you live on **Wilson Avenue.** Your neighborhood is called **Uptown.** Your city is **Chicago,** and your state is **Illinois.** The **United States** is your country. All these place names are nouns.

*How many nouns can you use to name things in this picture? Examples are **water, city, buildings,** and **streets.***

Now look around you. What do you see? Maybe you see a **desk,** a **crayon,** a **cat,** or your **bed.** Maybe you see some dirty **socks,** too! All these words are nouns. They are names of things.

CHAPTER TWO

COMMON AND PROPER NOUNS

DEFINITION

A **common noun** is a name for any thing within a group.

Do you have a pet? Or does your neighbor have a pet? What kind of animal is it? A dog or a cat? A fish, a hamster, or a frog? Whatever it is, that word is a common noun.

There are lots of dogs in the world. If you say **dog,** you can mean any of those dogs. So **dog** is a common noun.

Now—what is that pet's name? Springer, Mollie, or Lurch?

DEFINITION

A **proper noun** is a name for just one certain thing.

Springer is the name of just one certain dog. That makes **Springer** a

Here are three dogs that need names. What proper noun would you use for each dog's name?

This school's name is a proper noun. What is your school's name?

proper noun. And did you notice?

Springer begins with a capital letter.

If you say **school,** you can

mean just any school. So **school** is a common

noun. But **Taylor Elementary School** is one certain

school. And each word in this name starts with a capital letter.

CHAPTER THREE

ONE OR MORE THAN ONE?

A noun can be singular or plural.

Pencil, sticker,

and **box** are singular nouns.

DEFINITION

A **noun is singular** if it names just one thing.

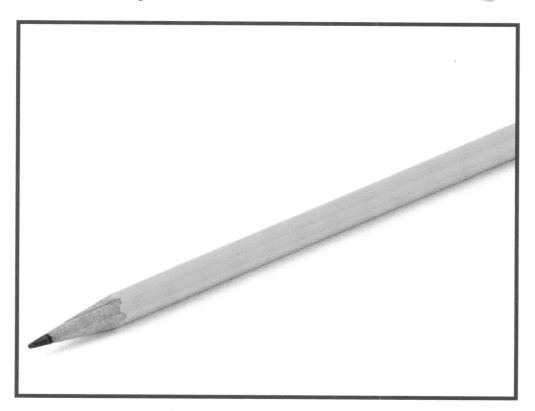

*This is just one pencil, so **pencil** is a singular noun.*

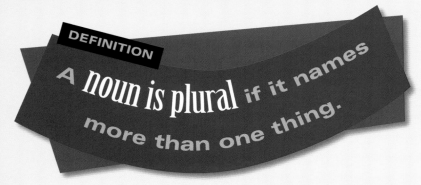

A noun is plural if it names more than one thing.

Pencils, stickers, and **boxes** are plural nouns.

How many pencils do you see here? **Pencils** *is a plural noun.*

Take the singular noun **box,** *add* -es, *and you have the plural noun* **boxes.**

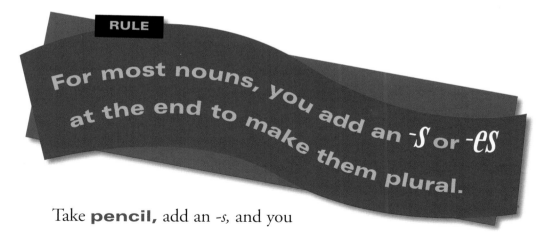

RULE

For most nouns, you add an -*s* or -*es* at the end to make them plural.

Take **pencil,** add an -*s,* and you

have **pencils.** Take **box,** add -*es,* and you have **boxes.**

CHAPTER FOUR

WATCH OUT FOR Y!

If a word ends with the letter -*y*, watch out! It might form its plural in a special way. How can you tell what to do? You have to look at the letter that comes before the -*y*.

RULE

If a vowel comes before the -*y*, you form the plural by adding an -*s*.

QUICK FACT

The vowels are a, e, i, o, and u.

Take the words **tray, monkey,** and **toy.** They all end with a vowel plus the letter -*y*.

Their plural forms are **trays, monkeys,** and **toys.**

Monkey has a vowel before the -y, so its plural form is monkeys.

If a consonant comes before the -*y*, you form the plural by taking away the -*y* and adding -*ies*.

*Fly has a consonant before the -y, so its plural form is **flies**.*

Now look at the words **baby, penny,** and **fly.** They all have

a consonant, or nonvowel, before the final -*y.* Take away the -*y* and

add -*ies* to make them plural. Then you have **babies, pennies,**

and **flies.**

CHAPTER FIVE

TRICKY PLURALS

N ow let's look at some tricky plural nouns.

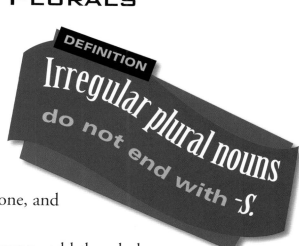

Irregular plural nouns do not end with -s.

Take a **child,** add another one, and

you have **children.** Take a **goose,** add the whole goose

family, and you have **geese.** Here comes a **mouse!** Along come

two more. Now there are three **mice.**

*These are not three mouses! They are three mice! **Mice** is an irregular plural.*

Children, geese, and **mice** are called irregular plurals.

They are plural nouns, but they don't end with *-s*.

TRY THESE!

You already know a lot of irregular plurals. What is the plural form for each of these nouns?

foot   elf   woman   tooth

See page 32 for the answers. Don't peek!

WATCH OUT!

Some nouns stay the same whether they are singular or plural.

Let's say a deer walked into your kitchen. You'd say, "There's a **deer** in the kitchen!" Suppose two more walked in. Then

you'd say, "There are three **deer**

in the kitchen!" The word **deer**

stays the same, whether it's singular

or plural.

These three deer are munching some delicious food.

17

CHAPTER SIX

MORE TRICKY PLURALS

WATCH OUT! Some nouns are plural, but they have no singular form.

Maybe one morning you get up and put on your pants. But would you ever put on just one "pant"? Of course not! There's no such thing as one "pant"! The word **pants** has no singular form.

Another example is **scissors.** You can cut paper with scissors. But you could never cut with just one "scissor." There's no such thing! The word **scissors** has no singular form.

*This girl is cutting with scissors. **Scissors** has no singular form.*

Other tricky plurals are **clothes** and **shorts.** They are plural, but

they have no singular form.

CHAPTER SEVEN

CAN YOU COUNT THEM?

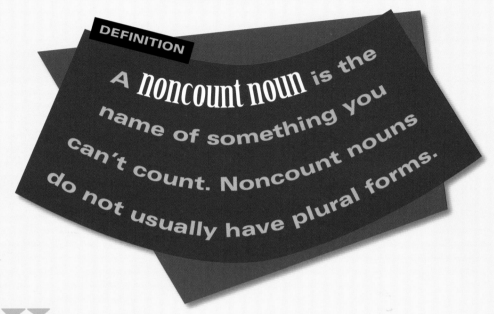

DEFINITION

A **noncount noun** is the name of something you can't count. Noncount nouns do not usually have plural forms.

You can count lots of things. You might count three cars, four glasses of water, and 10 balloons. However, you can't count traffic, water, or air. You would never say, "I see three traffics, four waters, and 10 airs"!

Traffic, water, and **air** are noncount nouns. They are names of things you cannot count. You would not usually use their plural forms.

You can count cars, but you cannot count traffic. **Traffic** *is a noncount noun.*

Many noncount nouns refer to foods or drinks. **Juice, milk, rice, cheese,** and **butter** are some examples. You might have three **glasses** of juice or three **bowls** of rice. However, you would never have five butters or nine milks!

You cannot count these nouns. They do not usually have plural forms. So they are noncount nouns.

HOT TIP

Try to count it. If you can't say "three whatevers," it's a noncount noun.

TRY THESE!

Which of these words are noncount nouns?

banana   fruit   soup   coat

wool   money   dime

See page 32 for the answers. Don't peek!

CHAPTER EIGHT

WHERE IS THAT GAGGLE?

Have you ever heard of a flock or a herd or a gaggle? These words are names for groups of animals. They are collective nouns.

A group of birds is called a **flock.** A group of sheep is a flock, too. Groups of elephants, cows, and deer are called **herds.** When geese get together, they're a **gaggle** of geese. Wolves roam around in a **pack,** and fish swim in a **school.**

Not all collective nouns are groups of animals. Some are groups of people. **Family, crowd,** and **class** are collective nouns, too.

> **DEFINITION**
>
> A **collective noun** is a name for a group of things.

This school of fish is exploring the sea for food.

Want More?

For more collective names for animals, visit these Web sites:

http://rinkworks.com/words/collective.shtml and

http://users.tinyonline.co.uk/gswithenbank/collnoun.htm

CHAPTER NINE

WHEN ARE TWO NOUNS BETTER THAN ONE?

DEFINITION

Some nouns are made out of two or more words. They are called compound nouns. Compound nouns join two or more things or ideas together.

Join **base** and **ball** together, and what do you have?

Baseball, of course! **Baseball** is a compound noun. It's an easy way to say "a ball game with bases."

Now, take **tea** and **pot.** Put them together, and you have a **teapot.** That's another compound noun. **Teapot** is a handy way to say "a pot that holds tea."

Butterfly is a compound noun. It's made from the words butter and fly.

As you see, compound nouns help us out. They give us a shorter way to talk about things. It's easy to see why people joined the words together.

TRY THESE!

- **What do you use to brush your teeth?**
- **What kind of book do you write notes in?**
- **Which room has a bed in it?**
- **What is a bird that's blue?**

See page 32 for the answers. Don't peek!

Some compound nouns don't seem to make sense. A **mushroom** is not mushy, and a **hamburger** is not made out of ham. A **butterfly** can flutter by—but it carries no butter!

DID YOU KNOW?

Some compound nouns are borrowed from other languages. For example, hamburgers are named after the city of Hamburg, Germany. People in Hamburg used to prepare a ground-meat food. When served in the United States, it was called Hamburger steak. Eventually, it was served in sandwich form and called a hamburger.

CHAPTER TEN

GET THAT ENERGY
OFF MY FOOT!

DEFINITION

A **concrete noun** is a name for something you can see or touch.

What are sidewalks made of? Most sidewalks are made of a material called concrete. Concrete is hard. Many concrete nouns are names for hard things, too. **Brick, chair,** and **penny** are concrete nouns.

Not all concrete nouns are names of hard things, though. Even a cool **breeze** and warm **sunlight** are concrete nouns.

If you can see, touch, or feel something, it's

HOT TIP

• Is it cold or hot?
• Does it have a color?
• Could you drop it on your foot? Then it's a concrete noun!

An *abstract noun* is a name for something you can't see or touch.

This girl is enjoying many things named by abstract nouns. They include happiness and fun!

a concrete noun. Maybe you can hear, smell, or taste it, too.

Do you have lots of **energy?** What's your favorite way to have

fun? Energy and **fun** are abstract nouns. You can have them,

but you can't see or touch them. And you certainly can't drop them

on your foot!

How to Learn More

At the Library

Browne, Philippa-Alys. *A Gaggle of Geese: The Collective Names of the Animal Kingdom.* New York: Atheneum, 1996.

Cleary, Brian P., and Jenya Prosmitsky (illustrator). *A Mink, a Fink, a Skating Rink: What Is a Noun?* Minneapolis: Carolrhoda, 1999.

Collins, S. Harold, and Kathy Kifer (illustrator). *Nouns and Pronouns.* Eugene, Ore.: Garlic Press, 1990.

Heller, Ruth. *Merry-Go-Round: A Book about Nouns.* New York: Grosset & Dunlap, 1990.

Terban, Marvin, and Giulio Maestro (illustrator). *Your Foot's on My Feet, and Other Tricky Nouns.* New York: Clarion Books, 1986.

Usborne Books. *Nouns and Pronouns.* Tulsa, Okla.: EDC Publications, 1999.

On the Web

Visit our home page for lots of links about grammar:

http://www.childsworld.com/links.html

NOTE TO PARENTS, TEACHERS AND LIBRARIANS: We routinely check our Web links to make sure they're safe, active sites—so encourage your readers to check them out!

Through the Mail or by Phone

To find a Grammar Hotline near you, contact:

THE GRAMMAR HOTLINE DIRECTORY
Tidewater Community College Writing Center
1700 College Crescent
Virginia Beach, VA 23453
Telephone: (757) 822-7170
http://www.tcc.edu/students/resources/writcent/GH/hotlino1/htm

To learn more about grammar, visit the Grammar Lady online or call her toll free hotline:

THE GRAMMAR LADY
Telephone: (800) 279-9708
www.grammarlady.com

Fun with Nouns

Choose the right collective noun for each animal group. You may use

flock, gaggle, herd, pack, or **school.**

1. A ———————— of geese

2. A ———————— of elephants

3. A ———————— of birds

4. A ———————— of wolves

5. A ———————— of fish

6. A ———————— of cattle

7. A ———————— of sheep

See page 32 for the answers. Don't peek!

Index

Answers

Answers to Text Exercises

page 16
feet
elves
women
teeth

page 22
The noncount nouns are: fruit, soup, wool, money

page 27
toothbrush
notebook
bedroom
bluebird

Answers to Fun with Nouns

1. gaggle
2. herd
3. flock
4. pack
5. school
6. herd
7. flock

About the Author

Ann Heinrichs was lucky. Every year from grade three through grade eight, she had a big, fat grammar textbook and a grammar workbook. She feels that this prepared her for life. She is now the author of more than 100 books for children and young adults. She has also enjoyed successful careers as a children's book editor and an advertising copywriter. Ann grew up in Fort Smith, Arkansas, and lives in Chicago, Illinois.

2 ''/06